Start with Art

Collages

Isabel Thomas

www.raintreepublishers.co.uk
Visit our website to find out
more information about
Raintree books.

To order:
☎ Phone 0845 6044371
📄 Fax +44 (0) 1865 312263
💻 Email myorders@raintreepublishers.co.uk

Customers from outside the UK please telephone +44 1865 312262

Raintree is an imprint of Capstone Global Library Limited,
a company incorporated in England and Wales having its
registered office at 7 Pilgrim Street, London, EC4V 6LB –
Registered company number: 6695582

Edited by Dan Nunn, Rebecca Rissman, and Catherine Veitch
Designed by Richard Parker
Picture research by Mica Brancic and Hannah Taylor
Originated by Capstone Global Library
Printed and bound in China by South China Printing
  Company Ltd

ISBN 978 1 406 22410 8
15 14 13 12 11
10 9 8 7 6 5 4 3 2 1

British Library Cataloguing in Publication Data
Thomas, Isabel
Collages. -- (Start with art)
702.8'12-dc22
A full catalogue record for this book is available from
the British Library.

Acknowledgements
We would like to thank the following for permission to
reproduce photographs: © Capstone Publishers pp. 5, 8, 10, 20,
21, 22, 23 – materials (Karon Dubke); Corbis pp. 9 (Albright-
Knox Art Gallery), 12 (© Images.com/Gerald Bustamante), 19
(The Art Archive); Getty Images p. 6 (Matt Cardy); Jo Brooker
pp. 7, 23 – fabric; Shutterstock pp. 11 (© Studio DMM Photog-
raphy, Designs & Art), 23 – gallery (© Shamleen), 23 – mosaic
(© tratong), 23 – self-portrait (© re_bekka), 23 – texture (©
Konstantin Sutyagin); Tate Images pp. 15, 18 (© Tate); The
Bridgeman Art Library pp. 4 (© Sarah Hammond. All rights
reserved, DACS 2011), 13 (Private Collection/© ADAGP, Paris
and DACS, London 2011/Giraudon), 14 (Private Collection),
16 (The Israel Museum, Jerusalem, Israel/© Romare Bearden
Foundation/DACS, London/VAGA, New York 2011/Gift of Mr
and Mrs Gerhard, New York), 17 (Roy Miles Fine Paintings/
Private Collection).

Front cover photograph of Trafalgar Square (collage) by
William Cooper reproduced with permission of
The Bridgeman Art Library (Private Collection).
Back cover photograph of a child looking through a magazine
reproduced with permission of © Capstone Publishers
(Karon Dubke). Back cover photograph of a child using glue
reproduced with permission of © Capstone Publishers
(Karon Dubke).

Errata
Please note the correct acknowledgement for
page 15 is Tate Images/© Barry Martin and
for page 18 is Tate Images/© Margaret Mellis.

Community Learning & Libraries
Cymuned Ddysgu a Llyfrgelloedd

This item should be returned or renewed by the last date stamped below.

To renew telephone: 656656 or 656657 (minicom)
or www.newport.gov.uk/libraries

ENRICHING
LEARNING IN
NEWPORT
SCHOOLS

ELIN	
Z778886	
PETERS	24-Jul-2012
702.812	£10.99

Contents

Some words are shown in bold, **like this**. You can find out what they mean by looking in the glossary.

What is a collage?

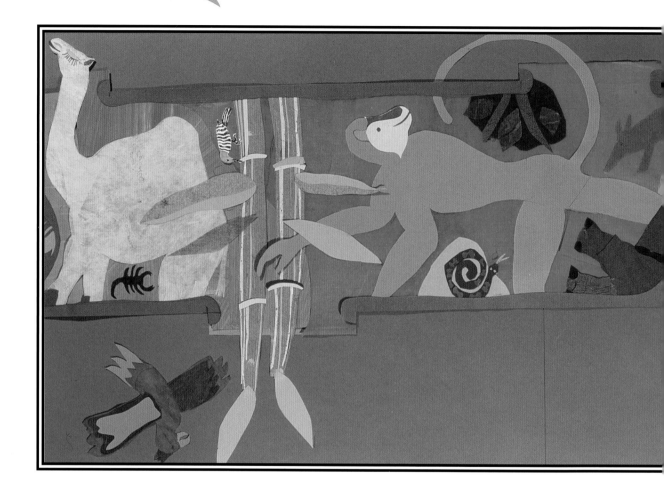

A collage is a picture made by sticking different things on to paper, canvas, or card.

Many artists make collages instead of drawing or painting.

You can be an artist, too.

A girl made this collage by sticking paper on to card.

Where can I see collages?

Some collages are displayed in museums and **galleries**.

Everyone can go and look at them.

You can see collages in books and magazines, too.

This collage shows you what the people in a story look like.

What do people use to make collages?

You can use almost anything to make a collage.

Cut or tear up paper, collect **fabric** scraps, and look for **materials** outside.

Try making art with things that would usually be thrown away.

This collage was made with old wallpaper, newspapers, and magazines.

How do people make collages?

Artists start by planning their collage.

They arrange different **materials** to make a picture.

When they are happy with the picture, they glue everything down.

This artist overlapped materials to give her picture **texture**.

How do people use shapes in collages?

This collage shows a picture of a flower.

The artist used rectangle shapes for the flower's petals.

Different objects have been glued on to paper to make this picture.

How many different shapes can you see in this picture?

What can collages show?

A collage can show real things.

Artists make collages of people, buildings, and objects.

Barry Martin '65.

Art can show ideas, too. This collage is about movement.

Can you spot a footballer's legs, a spacecraft, and an aeroplane?

How can collages show feelings?

Artists use shapes and colours to show feelings.

Grey, green, and blue colours make this picture feel calm.

Bright colours make us feel happy.

Which colours make you feel happy
in this collage?

What other types of collage are there?

Art can be very small or very big.

This collage is made from big pieces
of wood that washed up on a beach.

A **mosaic** is like a collage made
of small pieces of stone.

The Romans used mosaics
to decorate floors.

Start to make collages!

Many artists use newspaper and magazine clippings in their collages. Try making a funny **self-portrait** using **materials** you find.

1   Collect old magazines, newspapers, wrapping paper, and pieces of **fabric**.

2   Find a large picture to be the background for your self-portrait.

3 Cut a face shape and hand shapes out of coloured paper.

4 Cut a mouth, eyes, hair, and clothes from the materials that you collected. Arrange them to make a new picture – of yourself!

5   Add objects to show your favourite hobbies and toys.

6   When you are happy with your collage, stick everything down.

Glossary

fabric soft, bendy material, such as cloth. Clothes are made from fabric.

gallery place where art is displayed for people to look at

materials things you can use to make art

mosaic design made by sticking many small coloured squares together

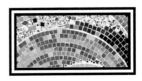

self-portrait picture that you draw or make of yourself

texture how something feels when you touch it

Find out more

Book

Action Art: Making Collage, Isabel Thomas (Raintree, 2005)

Websites

Visit this website to find more ideas for making collages:
kids.tate.org.uk/create/make_a_collage.shtm

Take a fun tour of modern art on this website:
www.moma.org/interactives/destination/

Index